one hundred
birthday wishes

one hundred
birthday wishes

ROHAN CANDAPPA

EBURY
PRESS

First published by Ebury Press in Great Britain in 2004

1 3 5 7 9 10 8 6 4 2

Copyright © Rohan Candappa 2004
All photographs © Corbis (except wish 86 © Rohan Candappa)

Rohan Candappa has asserted his right under the Copyright, Designs
and Patents Act 1988 to be identified as the author of this work.

Ebury Press
Random House • 20 Vauxhall Bridge Road • London SW1V 2SA

Random House Australia Pty Limited
20 Alfred Street • Milsons Point • Sydney • New South Wales 2061 • Australia

Random House New Zealand Limited
18 Poland Road • Glenfield • Auckland 10 • New Zealand

Random House (Pty) Limited
Endulini • 5A Jubilee Road • Parktown 2193 • South Africa

The Random House Group Limited Reg. No. 954009

www.randomhouse.co.uk

Papers used by Ebury Press are natural, recyclable products
made from wood grown in sustainable forests.

A CIP catalogue record for this book is available from the British Library.

ISBN 0091896940

Cover and interior designed by seagulls

Printed and bound in Singapore by Tien Wah Press

For my children, on their birthdays.

And every other day of their lives.

And for everyone else that I love.

Rohan Candappa lives in North London with his wife and two children. He never used to be any good at expressing his feelings. But he's getting better at it. This is his eleventh book. If you think you could do with a bit more laughter in your life you should give the other books a try.

introduction

How many words do the Eskimos have for snow?

The thing is, we don't tell each other what we feel. Not really. Not often enough. We skirt around the subject. We hint at it. We comfort ourselves with the thought that the other person 'knows how we feel about them'. It might be a partner, a parent, or a child. But whoever it is, we expect them to know.

Alternatively, we avoid the subject of feelings altogether. We shy away from sentiment, for fear of being sentimental. We save expressions of love for the heady realm of romance. Or the inadequate sign-off on a letter or a card. Or moments of crisis. And as for the love we hold for our friends, we are totally unequipped to express that in any way that adequately conveys just how much they mean to us.

The trouble is that 'love' is a word that's been stretched to cover so much. We can say 'I love my child' and we can say 'I love those shoes'. And in stretching the word so far, we have made it, in places, thin and brittle and prone to cracking. Until, when we do use the word, we run the risk of breaking it apart and finding ourselves standing knee deep in the splintered shards of what we mean to say.

At which point my mind starts to wander off in envy to the Eskimos – the Eskimos who, rumour has it, have forty-nine words for snow. They have so many words because snow is so important to their culture, their way of life, their very being. So what does it say about us that we only have one word for love?

Then I got to thinking that maybe if the word 'love' is too imprecise, too over-used, too easily misunderstood to use freely, then maybe it's other words that we need. Other words and an occasion when we are allowed to express just a small part of what we feel. Even if we don't know how to do it.

Every year everybody has a birthday, and all we ever tend to say on such occasions is 'Happy Birthday'. It occurred to me that 'Happy Birthday' is not enough, it's nowhere near enough, to express what I feel for the people I love. Of course, I do wish them a 'Happy Birthday', but I wish them more than that. I wish them so much more than that.

R.L.C

i wish you a shaft of sunlight on the gloomiest of days

1

2

i wish you a kiss
in the moonlight
from someone you love

i wish that no matter how much it rains your socks never get wet

3

4

i wish that no-one ever makes you eat brussel sprouts

i wish you friends who
love you for who you are

5

6

i wish you compassion

i wish you the sound of your children's laughter

7

i wish you the smell of new mown grass

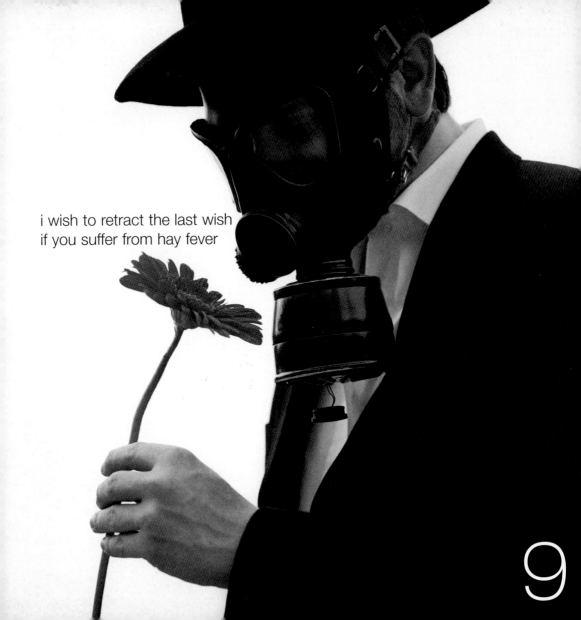

i wish to retract the last wish
if you suffer from hay fever

9

10

i wish that you never fear failure,
for doing so makes it hard to succeed

i wish you the strength to see the opportunities in your adversities

11

12

i wish you a mountain to climb and the will to do it

i wish you a big squashy sofa

with a cat sleeping on its arm

13

i wish that you meet someone who makes your heart race

i wish that you learn to tread lightly on the earth

15

16

i wish you the shade of a big tree on a sunny day

i wish that you never have to queue for the ladies loo

17

18

i wish you a
love of learning

i wish you the
temperament to teach

19

20

i wish that you never get caught in your zip
(or whatever the equivalent is for girls)

i wish that in restaurants you always choose the meal that everyone else wishes they'd ordered

21

22 i wish you a kingfisher darting low over a stream

i wish that no matter how venerable an age you attain, at least once a year you splash in a puddle 23

24

i wish you a long lie-in with breakfast in bed that sprinkles crumbs like confetti

i wish you never end up with anyone who snores

25

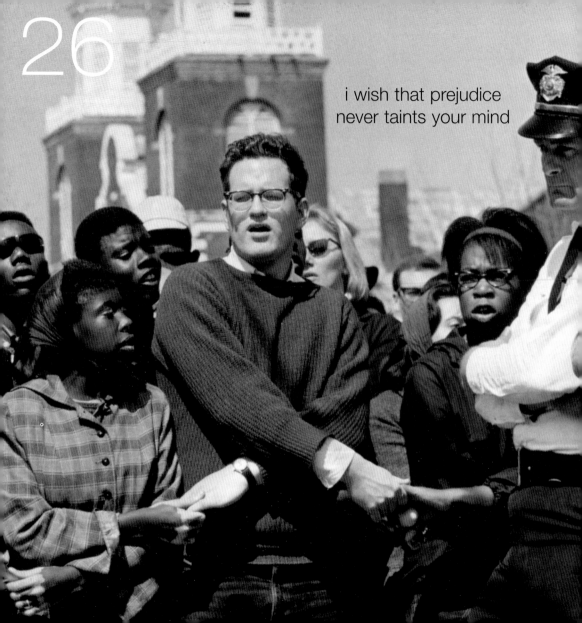

26

i wish that prejudice
never taints your mind

i wish you a home as welcoming as a mother's embrace

27

i wish you a hill to roll down on a sunny day

i wish that you see that beauty lies in the shadows as well as in the sun

29

30

i wish you the love of reading and a book at your bedside every night

i wish that you always
remember to turn the iron off

31

32

i wish you a dancing elephant

i wish that you never stub your toe

33

34

i wish you
hot meals
on cold days

i wish you cold drinks on hot days

35

36

i wish you rainbows and fireworks

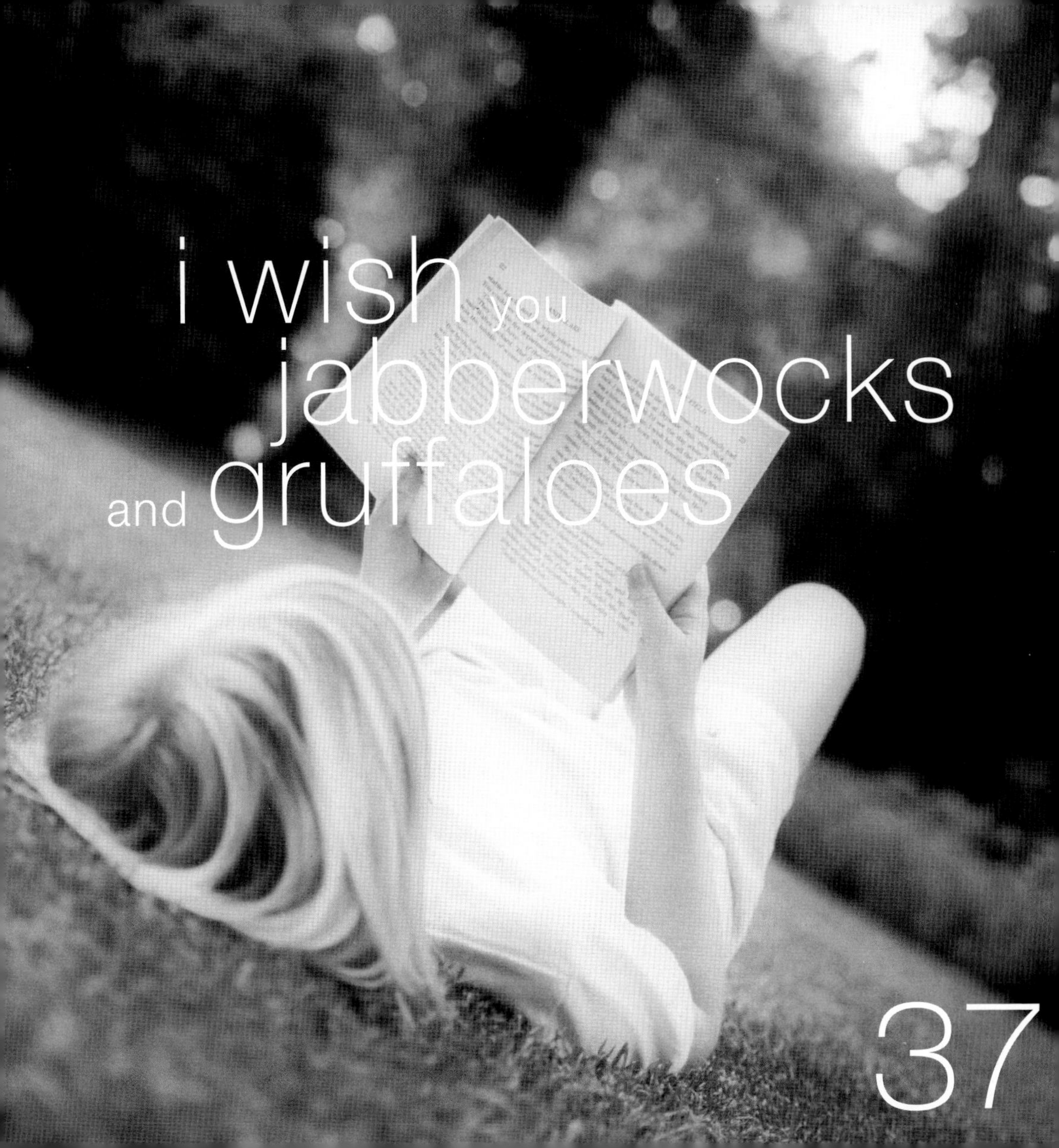

i wish you
jabberwocks
and gruffaloes

37

i wish you a good memory, except for grievances

i wish you the gaps between buildings and the worlds beyond that they reveal

39

40

i wish you a good plumber and a reliable builder

i wish that you know where the fusebox is whenever the lights go out

42

i wish that you learn that price
is rarely a measure of worth

i wish you
self-knowledge
devoid of self-importance

44

i wish that your gravy never goes lumpy

i wish that the bag never splits when you pull it out of the bin

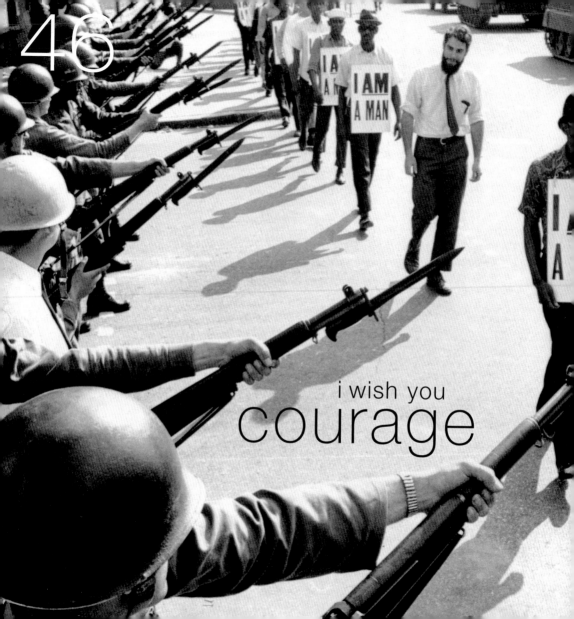

46

i wish you
courage

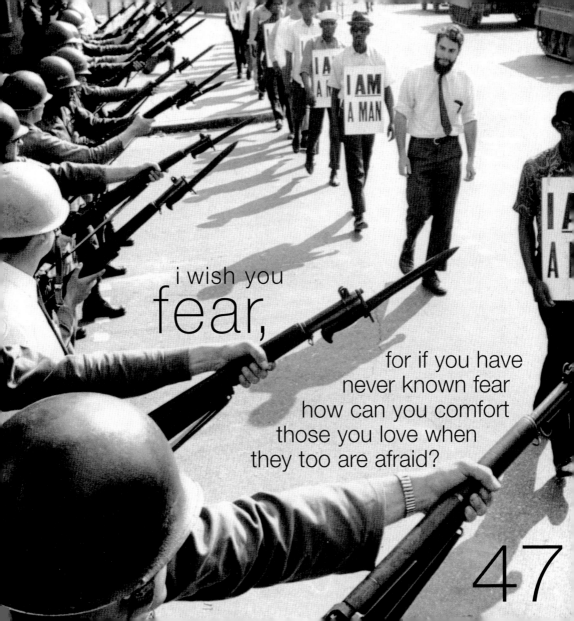

i wish you
fear,

for if you have
never known fear
how can you comfort
those you love when
they too are afraid?

47

i wish you ambition

never tainted by arrogance

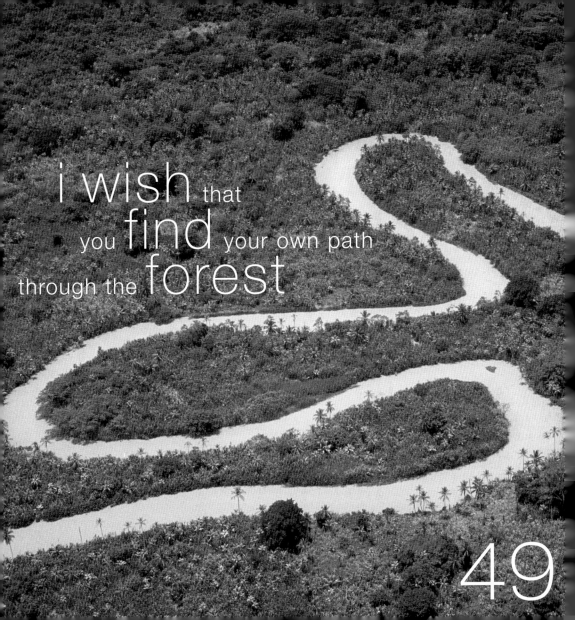

i wish that you find your own path through the forest

49

50

i wish you the sense to laugh at the world and all its absurdities and the wisdom to laugh at yourself before others do

i wish you mishtakes so that you can learn 51

52

i wish you patience, because
sometimes the world will insist
on walking when you want to run

Now
Serving
3

875

i wish that you always find your size, no matter how late you go to the sales

53

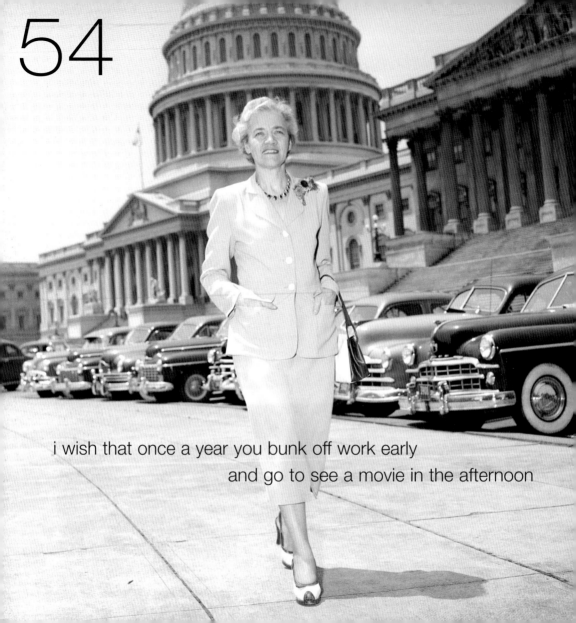

54

i wish that once a year you bunk off work early
and go to see a movie in the afternoon

i wish that no matter how many fancy restaurants you eat in

you never lose the love of a good bacon sandwich

55

56

i wish you the strength
to face your fears, to
recognise them as part of
yourself, and still move on

i wish you the wisdom
to listen to the inarticulate

57

i wish that you never lose the sustenance that is hope

i wish that a small child falls asleep in your arms

59

60

i wish you
a garden on a
summer's day
where two
squirrels play

i wish you two magpies wherever you go

61

62

i wish you confidence

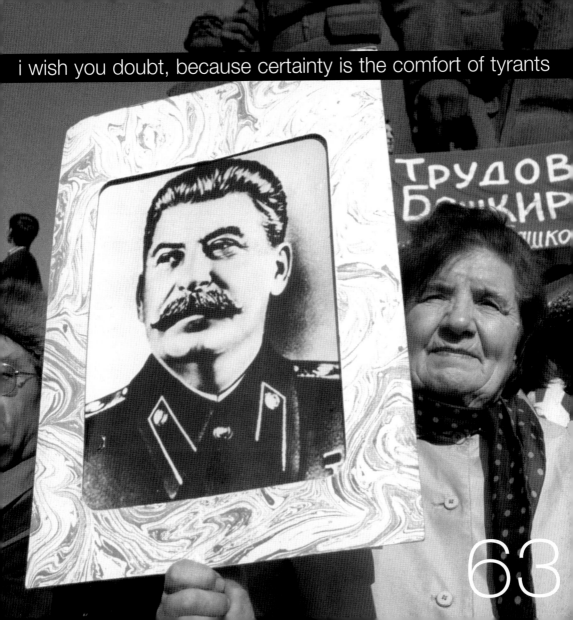

i wish you doubt, because certainty is the comfort of tyrants

63

64

i wish that your bread always
lands buttered side up

i wish that you're never the last to laugh

65

i wish that whenever you draw

you fill the page and use all the colours

i wish you choices

67

i wish you

clouds that billow like plumped up duvets

into the shapes of animals

and islands

i wish you
the fluttering wings of
hummingbirds
to lullaby you to sleep

69

i wish you passion

i wish that when you're blessed with old age you have memories to feast on and a mind that's still hungry

71

72

i wish that you're never too far from the next bun shop

i wish that you always have the time to watch a hesitant raindrop wending its way down a window pane

73

74

i wish you
birdsong

i wish that you remember all of us are flawed

and that's okay

75

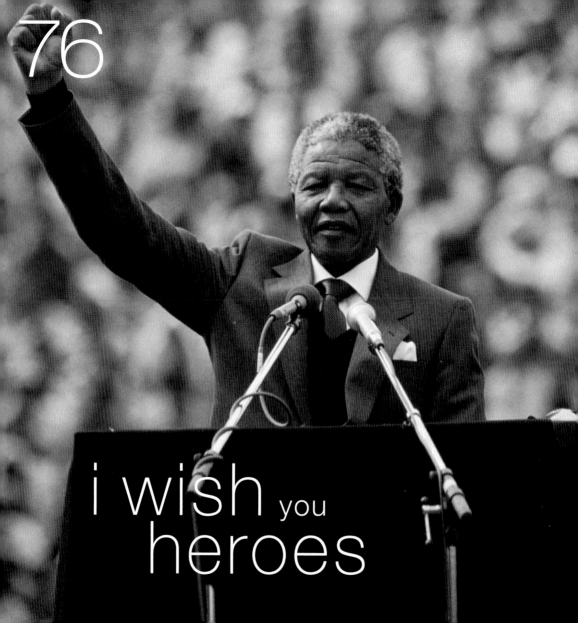

76

i wish you
heroes

i wish that no matter how tall you walk, you never look down on those around you

78

i wish you words that make you smile, like squelch, cous cous and jojoba

i wish that
what scepticism
you possess
never darkens
into cynicism

79

80 i wish you a
dennis bergkamp goal,
a nina simone song
and a glass of glenmorangie

i wish that
your dealings with lawyers
are mercifully brief

81

82

i wish that you learn that we have two ears
but only one mouth, for a reason

i wish you vision that lets you see the good in others

and the faults in yourself

83

84

i wish you the abandon to dance badly at weddings

i wish you always get a seat by the window

Photos

Passport
approved in
black & white
4 poses 80p
delivered in
4 min approx

i wish you
a passport
photo
that your
friends
don't
laugh at

i wish that you always make enough custard

87

88

i wish you a **boat** on an ocean that races with dolphins

i wish that you always help the woman with the buggy

89

90

i wish that eventually you always find the missing sock

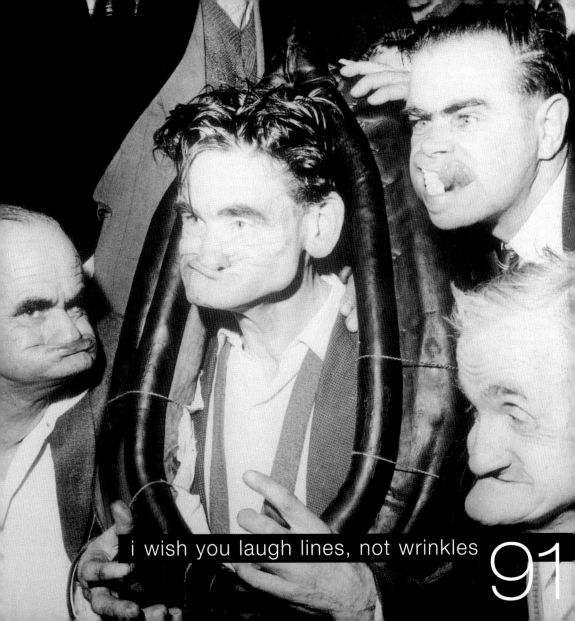

i wish you laugh lines, not wrinkles

91

92

i wish that even at your lowest ebb
you know that my love
is a turning tide that will
always find you

i wish that you always find money down the back of the sofa

94

i wish you daffodils every spring, snowdrops every winter
and the bluest of cornflowers every summer

i wish you snow on christmas day

95

i wish you the warmth of the beds that you slept in as a child

i wish you curiousity

97

i wish that you can feel my hand in yours whenever you need it i wish that you always have one wish left

99

i wish…

Also available by Rohan Candappa

To order please tick the box

☐ The Little Book of Stress £2.50

☐ Stress for Success £2.50

☐ Autobiography of a One Year Old £5.99

☐ Growing Old Disgracefully £4.99

☐ University Challenged £4.99

☐ The Little Book of Wrong Shui £2.50

☐ The Little Book of the Kama Sutra £2.50

☐ The Parents' Survival Handbook £3.99

☐ The Little Book of Christmas Stress £4.99

FREE POST AND PACKING
Overseas customers allow £2.00 per paperback

BY PHONE: 01624 677237

BY POST: Random House Books
C/o Bookpost, PO Box 29, Douglas
Isle of Man, IM99 1BQ

BY FAX: 01624 670923

BY EMAIL: bookshop@enterprise.net

Cheques (payable to Bookpost) and credit cards accepted

Prices and availability subject to change without notice.
Allow 28 days for delivery.
When placing your order, please mention if you
do not wish to receive any additional information.

www.randomhouse.co.uk